Pitching to Win

Strategies for Success

D1366233

Mindy Barker

Pitching to Win: Strategies for Success

Copyright © 2018 by Mindy Barker

ISBN: 978-1-61063-130-3
PCN : 2018956950
Printed in USA by OnLineBinding.com

Dedicated to my tenacious, creative, and genius clients – past, current, and future - who trusted with me with your journey to effectively increase the enterprise value of your company and raise capital. My passion is working with you. You have inspired me to write this book.

A special appreciation for Barry Banther, who coached me through the process of putting myself out there to write this book.

CONTENTS

1: Introduction

If you have picked up this book, you already know that building a business is a very difficult process. But did you know that when you need to raise capital, pitching to investors is not the same as presenting financials to a Board of Directors or in a town hall format? The Pitch requires a well-thought-out, strategic approach to prepare yourself and your enterprise to deliver an appeal that will convince investors to part with their money.

This book is primarily written for entrepreneurs who have arrived at the $1 million revenue mark or for executives with fundraising accountability. It can also be used by startups and more mature companies. The challenges in all cases are similar.

I love the world of entrepreneurship and have been exposed to it most of my life. My father moved my family from a small town in Georgia to Winston Salem, North Carolina, to start a company to metalize the egg-shaped containers for Hanes L'eggs Sheer Energy Pantyhose. The first summer after we moved, I had yet to make friends, so I worked in the factory, learning about building a business by watching my dad.

As entrepreneurs and founders, we tend to view our companies the way we view our first-born child. Every parent is convinced their child is perfect and could be the President of the United States, or something similar. This book has been written to help you and your enterprise by bringing you down to earth. As you read through the chapters, you may feel like you are reading one of the popular self-help books. The truth is, as with all leadership and executive positions, emotional intelligence and self-awareness are very important when strategizing and executing the process of pitching to investors and raising capital.

The pitch and the securing of investment dollars is not the end – it is the beginning of a business marriage. The strategic thought you invest on the front end of the process will help lead your enterprise to a successful partner who can assist you with company growth, not just simply write a check.

This book is written in simplistic terms, taking a holistic approach to the fundraising process. Having worked on both sides of the fence, one as a private equity professional and the other, company side, seeking to secure investment, I know that investors can seem like either your best friend or your worst nightmare. In general, they are narcissistic people who are extremely confident and can come across as intimidating. They can make you feel like you do not know what you are talking about. Keep in mind, that could be part of their due diligence process to test you. The fact of the matter is, if you expect them to invest in the growth of your enterprise, you need to prove that you deserve their investment by diligently preparing yourself and the team for this process.

In Chapters 1 through 6, I describe for you the tools to acquire from the beginning: your execution roadmap, organizational infrastructure, financial reporting, and relationships with potential investors.

Chapter 7 describes sources of funding, including some to avoid, while Chapter 8 examines how to find the right investors for you. Chapter 9 explains the importance of credibility. Chapter 10 walks you through building your pitch deck and how to behave during the delivery. In conclusion, Chapter 11 wraps it all up and tops it with a bow.

Throughout the book, I share tips and tricks, as well as the realities of the process. Knowing the challenges in advance will help you secure investment dollars. This is not a process I recommend for the faint of heart. You will hear criticism about your enterprise, and if you listen effectively, you may learn something that will help you grow your business. If you take the criticism personally and get defensive, you may lose investment dollars from someone who likes your enterprise but thinks you are immature.

The entire book is committed to obtaining capital for the best ideas, cocooned with the right infrastructure and the brightest C-Suite executives. Your ideas and vision that contribute to the day-to-day success of your great enterprise are what will propel you to success. By adding strategy and a thoughtful process to those great ideas, you will become a rock star in the world of securing investment.

2: Entrepreneur or "Lifer"?

It is hard to look at your business from an investor's perspective. Your life has been centered around the business, and you have put in tremendous blood, sweat, and tears. There are two different types of founders. One is an entrepreneur who may have begun with an idea and then moved forward to a proof of concept. This proof of concept has grown such that a business investor can see a clear path to invest money and grow it to make a return on their investment. The second is what I refer to as a "Lifer," who has an idea and has validated the proof of concept and developed a business heavily reliant on the Lifer.

Most founders and CEOs are certain their business is a good investment and that others should see it that way. Unfortunately, that is not the case in a high number of instances when we dive deeper into the aspects of a company.

Lifestyle Businesses Serve a Purpose

We each have a unique set of characteristics that drives us and puts us in situations where we are comfortable. Every time we make a choice to put ourselves in a situation and stay in it, something about that situation is working for us. Solid self-awareness and emotional intelligence help us make choices in life that work for all aspects of our lives and align with our relationship with money and our core values. A culture is developed around that. In business, the governance over this culture is ultimately driven by the purpose of the investors, shareholders, or founder(s). They determine the "Why" of the organization. Think of it as the driving passion for why the organization exists. More about the Why later in the book.

The culture and purpose of an organization can be several things. It can be a hobby, and you are okay with not making any money. I know many business owners who have built a lifestyle company that provides enough cash to pay their bills; they may also run all personal expenses through the company. They are examples of "Lifers." This practice is great if they happily accept the annual income they produce and do not have any desire to sell the company one day.

Entrepreneurs who are aware they need to build Enterprise Value will focus on establishing and monitoring metrics with the understanding they are building a business that can survive in the ecosystem of the investor world. They do not commingle their personal and business expenses. They listen to experts and focus on the important aspect of building a business. They may not take a salary from the business in the early years, opting instead to reinvest in the business and build a loyal customer base and revenue.

The problem arises when the Lifer wants to raise money from or sell the business to an investor – which really means they want the investor to fund their lifestyle.

MaryAnne ran an entrepreneurial business for years, employing family members throughout the business's history – a very common practice. One of her other business practices was to run family personal expenses through the business. On the outside looking in, it looked like a very profitable business that would be easy to sell. MaryAnne told me that many years ago she wanted to sell the business, having gone so far as to speak with a business broker. She was ready to sell immediately. What she didn't understand about selling a business is the due diligence process. Potential buyers want to see your financials. She knew that her business tax returns included the family's personal expenses. She thought it would be enough to explain her business to them and if they were interested, a deal would move ahead. That was more than five years ago. MaryAnne still owns the business and is still mystified as to why she has not sold it. By failing to consider and plan future scenarios of business ownership, she most likely will never find a buyer but will continue to live as a lifestyle business owner who dreams of someday selling her business.

Which Are You?

Before you get ready to pitch to investors, evaluate which type of business owner you are and if pitching to investors is the right thing for you. Do not waste your time and energy if it is not.

Use the following table to determine if you are an Entrepreneur or a Lifer:

Figure 1: Entrepreneur or "Lifer"?

Measurement Criteria	Entrepreneur	Lifer
Founder	Key employee	Key employee/Sole decision maker
Senior Leadership	Qualified/the best person for the job	People you trust – family and friends
Corporate Bank Account	Cash related to business expenses only	Cash includes business and personal expenses
Revenue	Planned and projected growth	Remains relatively flat
Financial Analysis	Financial strategy decisions made to build a business	Maintain balance to cover payroll and bills
Profits	Invested in the business	Distributed out to Founder
Balance Sheet and Cash Flow	Monthly analysis; discussed with trusted advisor	Seldom used
Planning	Comprehensive Budget, with communication/accountability throughout organization	Business Plan and forecast utilized principally by Founder and possibly for bank financing

Payroll	Processed by outside payroll source; taxes properly filed	Bookkeeper hand writes checks when money in the bank
Income Tax	Financial strategy planning with a trusted advisor; tax planning; proactive and healthy approach to minimize taxes	Avoids paying the taxes owed

Emotional intelligence and self-awareness are important to reach contentment in our life and business. If you determine you are a Lifer, do not go to others to raise capital, as you will spend a lot of time and energy only to arrive at a result that will likely not be what you expect. If you determine you are a Lifer who wants to become a career entrepreneur, engage the help of a trusted advisor to assist you with establishing the infrastructure to build Enterprise Value that attracts investors. Chapter 3 discusses building the Enterprise Value and what that means. It will take a great mindset shift, but if you have read this far without throwing the book across the room or putting it down, you have the stamina for it. If you are a Lifer and want to stay that way, embrace and love yourself and your company for that reality.

3: How Much Is My Business Worth?

The actual "value" of a business is what someone will pay for it. There are many examples of businesses, in both private and public markets, that are purchased for what a conservative number-crunching accountant would tell you is an insane amount of money.

Shipt, based in Birmingham, Alabama, was recently purchased by Target for $550 million, a huge valuation, as Target wanted the delivery system and infrastructure this company had developed to compete with Amazon.[1]

Amazon recently purchased PillPack for an estimated $1 billion to get into the healthcare market. The estimated annual revenue for PillPack is $20 million.[2] Anyone who has had to deal with medication management for a patient who takes a lot of medicine will realize quickly that PillPack has a valuable service to offer; but Amazon purchased it for far more than the intrinsic value would imply, at five times the annual revenue. PillPack's home office is in Somerville, Massachusetts. I mention where these companies are based because I find it encouraging and interesting that the entrepreneurial growth world is becoming more geographically diverse. This provides more opportunities for everyone.

No Entrepreneurial Easy Street

These examples of large valuations for entrepreneurial growth companies do not happen every day. Do not read one of the news articles about these acquisitions and then assume there is an overall Easy Street entrepreneurial growth lifestyle. You can be sure that the founders of all of these acquisition targets have their horror stories of the road they traveled. When a business gains traction in the entrepreneurial market with a proven concept, many firms will reach out to talk about working with you to raise capital, sell your business, or both.

Whether you are a rock star, or just a hard-working, flying-under-the-radar entrepreneur, banks, investment firms, and alternative lenders are getting incredibly creative with their marketing tactics to find companies to purchase and invest in. CEOs and founders may become exuberant and confident they are the next best thing since Uber – unicorn status is right around the corner in this market. Rock star!

These conversations often lead to discussions about high valuations, partnerships, and mentorship from the investment firm to help you grow exponentially. It seems that a glorious relationship is in the development stage.

Then, what happens next...

Investment firms and banks are run by people with whom you will be developing a trusting relationship. Be sure to keep yourself centered – this developing "friendly" relationship is about business. Your business will likely be held accountable under strict rules of governance. Lenders and investors must follow certain processes and procedures prior to sending you money. For this relationship to succeed, each partner must meet certain parameters in building the foundation, especially parameters related to your financials.

Here is the harsh reality. A number of these deals go "Poof!", up in smoke, due to inability to provide the investor or the bank with the right due diligence information. I recently met with a CPA firm to discuss ways we could work together. One of the partners said he has seen more deals with entrepreneurial growth companies and private equity firms fall apart lately due to lack of infrastructure. A business may appear to be solid, with a great growth trajectory yielding nice margins. However, the list of substantiating documentation required by investors is long, and the money people require you back up your claims with evidence such as:

- Customer records
- Accrual basis financials that are, at a minimum, up to par for a quality of earnings report, if not an audit
- Analytics of any one-off revenue-producing events that may have caused a spike in any given month
- Employee records, with signed copies of employment agreements
- Organized stock ledgers with all warrants, stock options, and stock equivalents available
- Material contracts, with signed copies and proper accounting for leases

Business owners who can produce this information have taken an important step toward rock stardom. Failure to produce these documents means that a deal with a lot of potential may quickly go up in smoke. Poof!

After the "poof," it hits you – while preparing for the due diligence process, sales may have dropped, and employees may have gotten wind of the potential sale and left the company. Employees who do not have an equity stake in the company see a sale as a threat to their future employment after the transaction. You are faced with building your company back up. The cost of not having the right reporting infrastructure and losing the deal will seem enormous at this point.

Selling your business may not even be on your radar, but consider this: What if someone approached you with an incredible price you would have never imagined, contingent on the due diligence process yielding favorable results? If presented with this opportunity, would your company be ready?

The way you look at your company financials for strategic decision-making is the same way that a buyer would look at them. By operating your business like it is going to sell tomorrow, you are more likely to be making informed decisions using timely, accurate data. If you aren't making informed decisions from your financial data, go ahead and get the kerosene and light the match, because it will all go up in smoke one way or the other.

Exuberance and overconfidence about your business can lead you to move away from core business principals and make decisions that are not the best for growing a business with a solid foundation that has infrastructure, goals, and metrics that can be measured and monitored. If you ignore these basic core needs, you are gambling instead of building a business. Enterprise Value must be created along with the growth of the business.

Building Enterprise Value

Enterprise Value is a financial term used often. It is the summation of the value of the equity plus the outstanding debt. The value of the equity is based on external factors and not the actual cash invested into the entity.

Enterprise Value is built over time with strong leadership and discipline. People, systems, and strategically-planned growth are all components of building great Enterprise Value. In the circle of the life of a business, it is all interconnected.

Remember, the value of a business is what someone will pay for it. Potential investors take the company's historical financial statements and apply traditional formulas to calculate the Enterprise Value or valuation, terms often used interchangeably. The value paid for a business could be *higher* than the valuation calculation if, for example, the buyer wants and needs a technology now but does not want to develop it. In the previous examples, Target purchasing Shipt and Amazon purchasing PillPack are examples of larger corporations needing the functionality and infrastructure successfully developed by the smaller companies.

The value paid for a business could be *less* than the valuation calculation if its people, systems, and processes are not transferable in a way that the new owner can build upon to scale the business, thus creating value. A Lifer may have an incredible product or service that attracts serious buyers; however, the valuation will be at a discount over what it would be for a similar entrepreneurial company if it has not been not built with a scalable infrastructure.

The value of a business is principally tied to a multiple of revenue, or EBITDA. This stands for "earnings before interest, taxes, depreciation, and amortization," and I will discuss how to calculate it later in this chapter. However, there is another step to determine how much money the buyer will have to expend to take over 100 percent of the business. Any debt must be paid off. You cannot call your banker and say, "Well, I just sold my business. It has been great working with you. Have a good day!" The bank is going to want to be paid; that must come out of the proceeds you receive upon the sale of the company or the buyer must pay it. There is a misconception among some sellers that the EBTIDA has a period, literally, after it. They assume they will take the sale money and the buyer will take over all debt, along with the warts of the company. Warts, yes; debt, usually no.

Market capitalization for public companies traded on the stock exchange is: current share price times total shares outstanding or owned by investors. The value created is based on the price the shareholders are willing to pay and can vary dramatically based on current events. Shareholders can be individuals, investment funds, or corporations. Their motivation to buy or sell could be due to recent news events, their own cash needs, or a recently-announced acquisition. Amazon is one of the most interesting companies to analyze when looking at public companies. In mid-2018, their market capitalization was projected to exceed $1 trillion. The acquisition of PillPack, mentioned earlier in this chapter, was a driving force of the surge in the price of Amazon's stock.

Privately-held companies have less ability to generate an immediate change in value. Their current investor base tends to be limited. The potential for new investors is dependent on the internal value created with the right people, processes, and systems.

Private companies typically engage with a potential investor to determine the value of a company with a discussion of EBITDA. Depending on the type of company, the multiple of EBITDA can be anywhere from 2x to 10x, but typically is in the 2x to 5x range. The following illustration shows how to calculate EBITDA:

Figure 2: Understanding EBITDA

Key = Each stack is equal to $10,000,000

A company generates $100 million in revenue and incurs $60 million in operating expenses.

Revenue:

Operating Expenses:

Depreciation and amortization expense is $10 million.

Depreciation and Amortization Expense:

This results in an operating profit of $30 million.

Operating Profit:

Interest expense is $5 million...

Interest Expense:

...leading to earnings before taxes of $25 million.

Earnings before taxes:

With a 20 percent tax rate, net income equals $20 million after $5 million in taxes are subtracted from pre-tax income.

Taxes:

Net income after taxes:

Using the EBITDA formula, we add operating profit to depreciation and amortization expense to get EBITDA of $40 million ($30 million + $10 million).

Operating profit + depreciation and amortization expense:

EBITDA =

When you consider the way businesses are valued, the reality is that loading your business with personal expenses and other tactics to avoid paying taxes is not a good strategy. To understand why, let's follow the conversation between Sally CPA and Ernie Entrepreneur:

Figure 3: A Tax Strategy to Avoid

Sally CPA: I see you added $1 of personal expense to your IS.

Ernie Entrepreneur: Won't that save me $0.30 on taxes because I'm in the 30% bracket?

Sally CPA: Yes, but if you try to sell your business or raise capital next year it will cost you.

Ernie Entrepreneur: Why? And how much will it cost me?

Sally CPA: This will lower your EBITDA, an important valuation tool by, by $1.

Ernie Entrepreneur: Why does that matter?

Sally CPA: Because it changes the valuation of your company in 4-6x EBITDA range.

Ernie Entrepreneur: Wow, I did not know that!

Sally CPA: So on average $1 of personal expense will cost between $4 and $6 of value.

Ernie Entrepreneur: Wow, that's a lot compared to my $0.30 tax savings!

Sally CPA: It is very important not to charge personal expenses to your business.

Ernie Entrepreneur: Good to know, thanks!

Ernie Entrepreneur   *Sally CPA*

There is an argument that personal expenses could be adjusted out when negotiating the price of your business, but it adds clutter to the conversation and does not paint your business practices in the positive light that you want. The math does not make sense if your company is an entrepreneurial growth entity. If you are a Lifer, your best-case scenario is to save your 30 cents and hope the IRS does not audit you. This kind of hope isn't a strategy I would recommend.

4: How Interconnections Build Value

Entrepreneurial leadership requires that you push yourself and your company forward. Strong, trustworthy connections with those who lead and run your company are foundational to building value over the long run.

As the leader, you set the bar for what you expect of yourself and your employees. Do you constantly focus on challenging yourself? How do you spend your time 24/7? Are you taking care of your physical and emotional needs? Are you listening to others' advice, and are you not afraid to ask for help when you need it? One piece of advice shared by experienced entrepreneurs is to surround yourself with people who are smarter than you.

Employee Interconnections

Your employees are a critical connection for pushing your company value forward. As a start-up, you may have employed friends and family to help get your business up and running. As you grew, perhaps they did not grow with the position or the requirements for the job were beyond their capabilities. Do not risk your business by keeping someone in a position that is not right for him or her. It is not only unfair to the employee, but it erodes the value of the business. Alternately, consider moving the employee to a different position. I have a client with a long-term employee who is a superstar in her third position with the company but who was a disaster in her first two positions.

The interconnection between trust and delegation cannot be overstated. Effective delegation – the opposite of micromanaging – is a skill crucial to leaders and managers. It requires a trusting interconnection between you and your employees. If you find it hard to effectively delegate, it may be because while you can give up control, you understand that you are still responsible for everything you just gave up. Take my advice on becoming a more effective delegator:

1. Work with people that you trust and have confidence in. Work diligently to build trust with your employees. Make sure you are listening to them. My maternal grandfather used to say, "There is a reason you have two ears and one mouth. Use them proportionately."

2. Let delegates know that they should feel free to come to you if they have any questions or encounter obstacles that will impact either the expected delivery date or quality need.

3. Develop enough self-confidence to let people fail – but encourage them to fail quickly so they can move on. We all have failed at one point or another; it is how you recover from failure and move on that matters. Ensure that the people with whom you work know this to be true from your words and actions.

Recognize that trust is a better virtue and will result in more long- and even short-term success than micromanagement. If you don't have trust, develop it. This requires you to hire and develop the right staff, as I have already mentioned. Trust is a two-way street, and you must admit your own failures to your staff if you want to build trust with them. You also must be forthright in your communication. You erode trust when you try to withhold information. Secrets have a way of becoming known. I have seen highly-divisive issues with acquisition integration at companies when employees have heard about a sale or merger on the street rather than from the leader of their organization. Acquisitions can be difficult to manage, as you do not want to tell employees until you are nearly certain it is going to happen. That is another reason you need to manage the process with potential investors, which will be discussed later.

Daily management of employees requires open communication, keeping conflict in check, and promoting a vision of each employee's future. These are all factors which, if not cultivated, undermine a company's value.

Successful managers share good and bad information. If you aren't the one telling employees the bad news and answering questions, they will create their own stories, which are often worse than the truth.

Part of open communication is acknowledging and resolving conflict. If two employees are at odds, everyone in your company notices, and productivity is undermined. Your failure to intervene due to a lack of comfort with conflict can mark you as wishy-washy. When all else fails, you may need to dictate the solution to resolve the conflict, ask both direct reports to honor your wishes, and eliminate the tension.

Training and development are key components of retaining the best employees, which leads to increased company value. An investment in employee education to achieve increased responsibility and the subsequent salary bump builds loyalty and retention.

External Interconnections

While leaders and employees are two critical components of an enterprise's culture, which is one of the drivers of value, the external influence of customers, partners, and vendors can undermine that value if strained relations exist.

My grandmother, who lived her entire life in North Georgia, used to say, "If you lay down with dogs, you are going to get fleas." How does that apply to vendors, business partners, and clients? It's about focus and the environment you want to cultivate within your organization.

To illustrate the impact of external relations, I will share this experience. A company I knew of repeatedly paid their vendors late or not at all. This wasn't due to failure to deliver goods or services, or other legitimate contractual reasons, it was due to the type of culture that existed in this organization. Two lessons stand out from this example.

First: Company employees knew this person wasn't paying the bills, yet they were still expected to deliver superior service. The leaders of this company were not taking quick, effective action to resolve the conflict, which served to undermine credibility.

Second: What would vendors say about this company? You can learn a lot about potential clients, vendors, and business partners through interconnections. As you consider going after investment dollars, what would your partners, clients, and vendors say to potential investors about their experiences with you? Would their testimonies withstand due diligence?

The bottom line is to make sure you have a razor-sharp focus on the culture you want to develop and the cultural and ethical boundaries beyond which you will not stray. If you are working with a customer or vendor who is not aligned with your culture and values, end the relationship and move on. A short-term loss of revenue will lead to a long-term gain in a more profitable way. It takes a long time to recover from negative energy, and the drain can keep you from accomplishing the end goal. Maintaining negative energy around you will dilute your ability to reach your company's goals.

5: Systems – Critical to Infrastructure

I was introduced to a company that was in the middle of finalizing a sale; the owner was ready to realize millions and still have an ownership stake in the business. During the due diligence process, cash flow slowed. The potential buyer became anxious, and the deal fell through. My gut told me the cash flow issue was probably due to the operational changes of one of their large customers; it was a timing issue rather than an actual loss of business. If the company's books and records had been organized so the data could support my gut feeling, perhaps the deal would not have fallen through.

Get to Know Your General Ledger

It is a fundamental concept of business accounting that the general ledger is where businesses maintain general financial information in a well-thought-out, organized way. The result is accurate records that can be efficiently analyzed and metrics to monitor the state of the company. In the worst-case scenario, a company will attempt to raise capital or sell the business, then will have to watch the deal fall through when the buyer or investors cannot complete adequate due diligence because of sloppy financial records.

I worked with a company that thought its revenue growth and ever-increasing gross margin was fantastic. The gross margin got so good that it seemed impossible. Further review showed that some products were not showing as released from inventory, and thus, a cost of goods sold. The situation was artificially inflating the gross margin – and everyone's optimism. When the audit was complete, the year that looked like a stellar year ended up showing a loss.

By establishing and maintaining good records on your customers, products, and lines of business, you will become aware of potential irregularities sooner rather than during an audit.

To stress my point, I'll share one more situation that could have been avoided with effective, routine financial reporting. I recently spoke with an entrepreneur who experienced an increase in business following a major hurricane. The business serviced buildings that had been affected during a hurricane. The company was growing significantly prior to the hurricane; however, there was a large growth surge during the storm. The founder was seeking investment dollars for growth in the company, and investors were having a hard time distinguishing between the business increase due to the hurricanes and whether the growth would have happened under any circumstances. They were concerned that if you stripped the hurricane business away, the business would not have grown. The founder was totally convinced his business was in growth mode despite the hurricane but was unable to prove it in a manner to satisfy investors.

Proving growth or understanding if product lines are making or losing money comes from correctly configuring the general ledger, then correctly applying transactions. Some companies unprofitably run segments, locations, and lines of business for years because they do not maintain the books and records that would show these things are unprofitable.

The solution is to set up a general ledger with segments to help identify and allocate revenue and expenses. It is much harder to go back and allocate historical information once it is in the general ledger a certain way.

For example, if you pay rent for a manufacturing location that makes four products, and the machinery for each product takes up an equal amount of floor space, then you can divide rent and utilities four ways. If each product has a supervisor, then the cost of the supervisor associated with each product should be allocated to their product. Begin with the actual expenses and work line by line to determine how they should be allocated.

Revenue by location, segment, line of business, etc. is generally much easier to break down. If a portion of the revenue is difficult to break out, you should assume and allocate based on something. For example, if you sell warranties for your products and have not kept up with the warranty revenue for each product, then allocate it based on the percent of sales revenue of that product to the total revenue for products that are warranted.

Strategically-Planned Growth

The key to survival is measuring and monitoring the results. It is essential to complete an annual budget, break it down into monthly components, and monitor each month. The budget should include an income statement, balance sheet, and cash flow. Most companies have an income statement; however, I have seen fewer balance sheets and cash flow projections. This can really get you into trouble, especially if you have inventory on your balance sheet.

In addition to a budget, a company should have a business plan and a five-year forecast. The business plan should articulate the plan for the company's growth and address anticipated changes in the economy and future trends. It is difficult to predict all these things, but if you develop a robust business plan, you are thinking through the different scenarios and how these scenarios will impact your business.

The projections should reflect what you really think the business can produce within the specified time frame. The calculations should have some basis in reality. Document your assumptions, even if only for yourself, so that as assumptions are confirmed or adjusted you can re-project. I have rarely seen revenue the first year after an investment is made equal the projected revenue. This is a shame, as the result may be an uncomfortable conversation with your new partner and investor on why. Be realistic about your sales cycle and your current pipeline. If your sales cycle is typically 12 weeks, you have $2 million in the pipeline and you typically close 50 percent of your pipeline, there is no way you are going to close $5 million in business in the next quarter. I have worked through this kind of basic math with business owners before, and many still unrealistically expect that one large client they do not know about today will come to them and close so they can meet that projection. That is not good business – that is gambling. Do not do it.

I worked with an organization a few years ago that historically had double-digit growth each year and was very profitable. The initial product the business launched was a great success, much better than anything on the market. The company was getting ready to launch a second product, and at my first management meeting, we discussed how the product was already on its way to the warehouse. As an incentive, they offered extended terms to customers on their entire order if the new product was added. No one had projected the effect this would have on the balance sheet and cash flow. This move would essentially stop incoming cash, yet they had just signed up for a huge payable to the vendor. The company had to react quickly to manage cash for payroll and other obligations. It ran cash flow projections daily during that time.

With an effectively-constructed general ledger, budget, and business plan in place, you are ready to make them work for you by keeping you apprised of the state of the company. A company dashboard can serve as the early warning system and report card on how things are going so that you can act sooner, rather than later, as these previous examples illustrated.

6: Create Your Company Report Card

In my experience working with new clients, I have developed a proven process that I follow to uncover the true pain points of a business. When I begin, I review the financial statements and then meet with the stakeholders to determine what they think about the business and its success. The stakeholders are generally the leaders of the company. Their stress level is one of the most important metrics of a business. They could be stressed about cash, the balance of debt, employee turnover, the number of sales calls made each day, or some other metric.

In some cases, it turns out stress is caused by lack of information. Stakeholders don't know where to focus their stress, so they worry about everything. This is where a company report card can help channel and focus the stress, ultimately leading to corrective actions.

The company report card can be a daily dashboard, a weekly or monthly flash report, or a month-end financial report. Managing the stress of the stakeholders is dependent on having clear and concise information about the things they have historically been concerned about and the things I educate them they *should* think about.

Elements of the Company Report Card

There are hundreds of metrics to consider when developing the tools to monitor a business. I often chuckle inside when I meet with a potential client. Before I even get to know them, they may ask what metrics, or Key Performance Indicators (KPIs), I would calculate for them. If you simply want a basic template and Excel spreadsheet, you can go to Google. If you want a strategist who helps the team understand the business in a healthy way and move it forward to be the best it can be, then let's do it. Listening and paying attention to the way a business is run can determine the best measures to track and increase the value of the business.

Below is a sample of metrics you can establish and maintain to track company performance. With some forethought, metrics can be captured and changed out as your company progresses through different stages of maturity.

The Stress Level of the C-Suite. Depending on your company culture, you may ask each leader to provide a number between 1-10 to the group, with 10 being the most stressed. Evaluate what each leader attributes as the cause of his or her stress level, then work together to manage and maintain a lower stress level. Ultimately, the collective lower stress can lead to more productive, clear-thinking minds. Stressed leaders do not make effective leaders, and that stress flows downhill, affecting those who work for you. An abundance of information, in a variety of formats, is available on stress management techniques.

Revenue. Top line revenue should be measured and monitored, as well as sliced and diced. If you offer a variety of products, you need to look at the revenue produced by each.

Cost of Goods Sold and Inventory Levels. I am combining these concepts, as they should be reviewed together. Too often, projections and metrics are based on the cost of goods sold, but you must have a product to sell. For example, inventory could be an issue if you are selling a software service that requires hardware and you are supplying the hardware to the customers as they sign on as a customer. If your inventory of hardware drops, sales of your software service will suffer if it is hardware-dependent.

Manage inventory to a number that works with the cyclical nature of your business. I have a customer who does about 30 percent of sales during the holiday season. To manage the fluctuation in demand, he rents extra warehouse space in October to begin stocking up for the season.

People and Salary Metrics. The number of employees per revenue dollar is one of the metrics investors like to review. Staff turnover is a metric that managers and their leaders should review. Salary and benefit expense can get expensive fast. Combine that with a high turnover rate, and replacing staff causes those expenses to skyrocket. Avoid the tangible and intangible costs of turnover by investing in your staff. Depending on open positions you need to fill, the expense can range from $15,000 to two times the base salary.

Expenses. Establish a budget and projections for all your financial statement items, but also have very detailed and well-thought-out budgets for expenses. Areas in which to pay especially close attention are contracts for rent, lease of equipment, and software subscriptions. The key to avoiding unplanned expenses is to make sure you understand the renewal rates and escalation clauses. Vendors are masters at getting you interested in their product with low monthly upfront costs, but not explaining the total cost of ownership.

Case in point: I recently had a case where the first-year renewal for the customer relationship management software (CRM) was almost three times what was in the budget and what had been anticipated. To avoid this type of surprise, each expense should have a professional who will monitor the expense throughout the year, anticipating when it will be incurred. Avoid having to communicate with investors and major stakeholders about why there were increased expenses due to unexpected bills. Surprises are great at birthday parties and on Christmas morning, but not so great when you are going over financial statements with investors.

Cash Flow Management. A 12-week rolling cash projection is an invaluable tool for growing companies to keep all necessary stakeholders aware of cash balances, overdue customer accounts, upcoming cash requirements, and other cash-management items. The 12-week rolling cash should be formatted in a summary manner. This cash flow is not the same as the cash flow in a GAAP-audited financial statement. Fast-paced executives need a concise and systematic way to remind them, at-a-glance, of the items they consider most critical for decision-making and performance monitoring. A well-thought-out, high-level summary on one page allows you to see if there is a negative balance on the horizon. An accountant can dig into the details and determine what is causing the issue and propose at least two options to cure the cash overspend. By "managing up," you can mentor your accountants to consider the perspective of their customer – most importantly, the C-Suite and the board.

One of my CEO clients told me they had to liquidate hundreds of thousands of dollars of personal assets to raise cash for payroll a few weeks prior. When I asked to see the cash flow report, I received a report in eight-point font covering four pages of exhaustive details. Unless a CEO has two full days to devote to diving into cash flow, there is no way they are going to understand the status if they receive something of this nature. I have not met many CEOs who have that kind of time to spend. CEOs expect succinct reporting to guide them in making thoughtful and informed decisions. Leave the details for those who must dig in and uncover issues.

With thousands of metrics available, if you aren't sure which to use, choose metrics that apply to the way you or potential investors think about your business. Do not create a dashboard that takes on a life of its own, requiring a full-time professional to maintain, if you are not going to use it effectively. I am frequently shocked at how much time is spent putting together information and reports that no one ever sees. Make sure you use the time of all professionals effectively. Think strategically about how to set up, manage, and monitor metrics. Train anyone who contributes input on how their actions impact what is ultimately reported.

7: Show Me the Money!

Develop a Strategy

The decision to raise capital should be preceded by establishing a business that is building Enterprise Value. From that point in a business's maturity, you are creating the value of the business. Once you have determined that capital is required to increase the value of the business, you must then begin to strategize about how to raise the capital.

In this chapter, I describe the approach to raising capital and the different types of sources. Your strategy will depend on the goals you target.

The first step: start with the end in mind and think through what you want – both short and long term. Do you want to completely exit the business, or just take some chips off the table and diversify your assets? Who are you willing to sell your business to – a strategic or a financial buyer? Do you want to continue working full-time, now or in the future? The answers to these questions can guide you to the capital sources that can help you meet your goals.

Funding Alternatives

There are different stages of fundraising; historically, the different sources of capital are associated with one of these stages, as demonstrated in the following table:

Figure 4: Comparison of Funding Source Alternatives

	Funding Alternatives			
Stage	Traditional	Most likely	Investment Alternatives	Debt Alternatives
Seed Capital – Startup phase	Founder Funds	Friends and Family	Venture Capital	SBA or other government-backed financing, with personal guarantee
Series A – proven business model and plans for growth	Venture Capital	Friends and Family	Private Equity or Family Office	Factoring or Line of Credit, with personal guarantee
Series B – significant growth and infrastructure established to	Private Equity	Family Office	Venture Capital or Strategic Buyer	Factoring, Line of Credit, Traditional Bank

Funding Alternatives				
Stage	Traditional	Most likely	Investment Alternatives	Debt Alternatives
further growth				Financing, usually without personal guarantee
Series C – E or IPO ("Initial Public Offering")	Public Stock Market	Private Equity or Strategic Buyer	Family Office	Factoring, Line of Credit, Traditional Bank Financing, usually without personal guarantee

Recently the lines have blurred, as flush venture capital, private equity, and family offices have sought alternatives in which to invest their stockpiles of cash. The overhang of capital held by these fund sources has become an issue to the point where they need to invest the money for their own survival. These entities raise funds and enter into partnership agreements with limited partners, where they commit to invest the money over a certain number of years. Some of the money that remains in these firms today was raised five years ago, which is about the average time in which these partnership agreements require the funds to invest the dollars. Complicating this dynamic, the debt market has shifted back to the crazy-town low bar for providing cash that existed pre-recession. I recently spoke with a CPA firm partner who said, "I thought I would never see this again. They are giving out money and closing loans just like the 'good ole' days.'"

One option not listed above is usually the first option to consider if you have not already – that is to significantly change your lifestyle and spend your own money to raise the capital from your own savings, 401k, or equity in your home. However, the decision to leverage your family's financial stability to pursue entrepreneurship should not be taken lightly. The investment of your time and money will cause stress, taking a toll on your family life. You must be clear with your family when considering such a move as to how long this could last and what the endgame means to them as sideline stakeholders. Make sure you have their buy-in and support. Going through marital discord while you are building a company is not recommended.

The sources to raise capital outlined above each lead to a different life of the company and different lifestyle and expectations for the founder. How do you decide which one is the best option for you? Some of the factors to consider when choosing a source of capital are: how rapidly do you want to grow your business? Is your product or service attractive to venture capital? Do you have the desire to give up equity to private equity, venture capital, or major investors? Are you willing to risk relationships to have family and friends invest in your company?

Giving up equity is an emotional choice, and you need to get your mindset appropriately calibrated before you initiate this process. The possibility of someone giving you a lot of money to build and grow your business without expecting a substantial chunk of the equity in return is small. By having candid conversations with entrepreneurs who have gone down this path before, you can get a better understanding of what it means to give up equity, and what they would have done differently, given the chance. Surrendering equity should come with a strong partnership that will lead you to believe a smaller portion of a big pie is better than keeping a large percentage of a small pie that is not going to grow.

Funding Pitfalls to Avoid

When you are ready to proceed with seeking sources for capital, consider that each source has associated pros and cons. I've provided some of the pitfalls you can face with each source to help with your decision-making.

"Friends and family" may seem like a "comfortable" option for you as you raise your business. They know how smart you think you are; they know that you are wonderful and have the brains, tenacity, and perseverance to make this incredible entrepreneurial company the most fantastic organization ever. They will get so excited about your idea and, as if you are the Pied Piper, will follow your entrepreneurial journey every step of the way. It all sounds so enticing and comfortable because you'll be surrounded by a warm blanket from your grandmother's house as you build this business. You know that your entity will make an incredible amount of return if you just had the capital to spend, and you will be happy to share with your family if they help you with the investment to gain the momentum. You began to share the excitement with family and friends, they buy into it, and they are willing to invest. They may even be willing to mortgage their house for a lot of money to help you with this incredibly awesome endeavor. You all agree you may get the money from them without genuine shareholder agreements or documents, and you may even take money before you even have a corporate agreement. I mean, it's only your friends and family, why does it matter? You trust each other, you have a great relationship, it's a great idea – in fact, it is a match made in heaven. What could go wrong?

Let me tell you what can go wrong. From the first decision you make about how to spend the money, friends and family investors will be looking over your shoulder. Each person makes different decisions based on their relationship with money and current circumstances – decisions such as whether you can pay yourself and how you will pay the bills such as the corporate credit card and rent, to having enough recurring revenue from customers to cover all expenses. These are very difficult decisions each entrepreneur will face when they review their bank account and look at cash. Are you prepared for friends and family to question why you decided to spend money one way versus another? Will you feel obligated to show them the details, such as how much was spent on your salary, travel expenses, marketing expenses? All those costs can be questioned by outsiders looking in. I can absolutely guarantee you that as an entrepreneur when you are in the early stages of a business, you will have a difficult time deciding how to spend money. The decisions you make may not fit what your investor would have done. If you are dealing with an arm's length investor, it is easier to work this out than it is with family. Every family is dysfunctional, and having your father-in-law or other family member invest in your business will most likely create stresses of this type.

Friends and family generally invest either prior to company formation or in the early stages. If you decide to accept money from this source, take the time to meet with a qualified attorney to set up the proper corporate documents. These steps can help avoid uncomfortable situations that could arise because of the relationship.

If the company is just being founded, consult with the CPA who prepares your tax return to determine which type of entity works best for you and the organization you are creating. Ask the investors who are providing the capital their preference, as well. Make sure that corporate documents include governance directives addressing how the money is going to be spent. For example, you may require the Board of Directors to approve all expenditures over a certain dollar amount.

Additional Funding Sources

If, after reading the preceding, you decide not to risk relations with family and friends, angel investors are a great way to build a business. Angels are typically high-net worth individuals who have made their money by cashing out on a previous business, by having a corporate job where they earn equity, or sometimes by being an individual from a wealthy family. Depending on their background and their expertise, they can be an incredible resource for you as you build your business. The problem with finding these angel investors is they typically don't walk around telling everybody they have money to invest or broadcasting via their favorite social media page, "Hey

– I would love to spend millions of dollars on an entrepreneurial private business." They tend to hide underneath a rock within the community and discretely seek ways to invest.

Finding such angel investors requires you to develop a trustworthy network within the entrepreneurial growth community and communicate to others your interest in finding investors. Think of building this network as an investment because your initial tendency may be to feel like these people are wasting your time. Listen more than you talk so you can go away with some nugget of information or an idea on how to effectively grow your business. Some angel investors only want to invest in specific types of businesses. You can effectively network by pre-qualifying those you meet to make sure their interest aligns with the type of company you have.

In some respects, working with angels can be less stressful than other sources when building your business. But keep in mind, they may not be as helpful as venture capitalists in offering advice, finding customers or new management, or cultivating the company's reputation. Angels do not have the infrastructure to help you with raising additional capital, and you may have to start all over when you grow past this round of funding to seek more.

Venture capital has traditionally been an investment market for information technology and other tech-type companies. VCs tend to invest in technology that they think will rapidly grow and take off in a manner to quickly make a lot of money. The typical investment of up to $10 million has an expected holding period of four to seven years. The investment vehicle tends to be all equity (common stock) and is not typically a majority stake, at less than 50 percent ownership. These investments can have some of the more sophisticated finance vehicles attached to them, such as warrants and options.

Venture capital firms tend to focus narrowly on one type of company. Regardless of whether you intend to raise capital immediately or not, always have some idea of which venture capital firms focus on your industry. Periodically review the investments they are making and the topics of articles they are posting on LinkedIn and other social media platforms, and attend in-person networking events the professionals may attend. You will learn a lot about the industry you are in and your competitors. Some of the ways to get information about venture capital firms are from their websites, YouTube video posts, Ted Talks, and professional journals.

Private equity (PE) has traditionally been a market for later-stage companies. PEs tend to invest in a variety of industries, not just IT and tech-type companies. The typical investment range is $10 million and up, with an expected holding period of six to 10 years. These firms can invest through equity (preferred stock) and debt (loans). A typical investment vehicle is convertible preferred stock, a form of stock used to raise funds. Private equity firms select investments because they feel they have the expertise or they can tuck in the acquisition with one of their existing portfolio companies and generate synergies for growth.

Historically, corporations have not been the typical source to seek an investment or execute a full exit strategy. Corporations set up their own Merger and Acquisition departments (M&A) to seek opportunities to purchase technology, customer bases, and infrastructure they need but do not have the time or expertise to build in support of their overall strategy. Corporate M&A departments can make a partial investment in your company, which could allow you access to their large corporate infrastructure and expertise when structured to do so. It will also build a relationship that may allow for a full exit strategy. The following story is a good example.

When Swiss healthcare giant Roche acquired Flatiron Health, it represented the marriage of data and technology to help advance cancer treatment. In a press release, Nat Turner, Flatiron Health Co-founder and CEO said, "Roche has been a tremendous partner to us over the past two years and shares our vision for building a learning healthcare platform in oncology ultimately designed to improve the lives of cancer patients. This important milestone will allow us to increase our investments in our provider-facing technology and services platform, as well as our evidence-generation platform, which will remain available to the entire healthcare industry."[3]

Family offices are private firms that manage investments for wealthy families. They may be a potential investor and partner to grow a business. This can work especially well if the family businesses are in the same industry as your company. However, family offices typically do not have the full infrastructure a private equity or a corporate entity will have to help you grow the business.

The criteria that surround the different capital sources should be considered carefully before you proceed forward. Having the right set of facts and figures to provide to any potential sources of funding is as important as who you are approaching to initiate the "investment conversation."

If you choose to raise money from outside sources, you as the entrepreneur must first get your mindset in the right place to move forward. Recognize it can take up to three times longer than what you think it will. Raising money and running your business at the same time can be difficult. Accept that you will hear things about your business that may not necessarily feel all that good; it will be difficult to accept feedback as constructive criticism and not take it personally. The final thing you must wrap your head around is this: you must give away some of the equity in your company to achieve your bigger goals.

8: Speed Dating for Entrepreneurs

Or: How to Screw Up a Relationship

You never know who you are talking to, and it can happen anywhere: you may be having a conversation with the perfect investor and be screwing it up. Avoid just such a disaster by approaching each conversation about your business with the most emotional intelligence you can develop. And have key information at your fingertips to help know who you are speaking with.

We spoke about the right kind of infrastructure, including a CRM. One of the uses of your CRM is as a business-intelligence gathering tool. By creating a separate segment from potential customers, you can store business intelligence on potential investors. Include details such as each time you are in contact with them, what you discussed, and any follow-ups. Take a proactive approach by sending them a high-level executive summary periodically about your business, even prior to needing their money. It is best to develop a relationship with this group prior to the need for using them to raise capital.

True experience: I am often asked how to find the right investor to invest in an entrepreneurial business. The question often comes from an entrepreneur who is about to run out of money and wants me to introduce them to someone who will write them a check by the end of the week. For the investor/entrepreneur relationship to work effectively, a relationship of trust and understanding must be cultivated during the pitch and due diligence process.

Would you ask a friend of yours, on Monday, to introduce you to a spouse you can marry on Saturday? I hope not! So why would you think an investor relationship would work that way? The message you are sending is, "I'm a poor planner and waited until I was in trouble to take action." Not a good way to start a relationship that involves asking for money, is it?

As with any business relationship, finding the right fit with an investor is the first step in a long and successful association. This may sound like dating advice, as there are many similarities. For example, identifying potential investors through word-of-mouth or introductions from mutual friends has a better chance of success than selecting the first name your search engine delivers.

But don't stop there, ask your acquaintance *why* they recommend one investor over another. It is critical that whoever you choose to ask for money understands your goals.

With potential candidates on your list, think of a few "speed dating" questions to narrow the list down. Know yourself well enough to already know which questions/answers would be deal-breakers. What does that mean? Let's say you want a silent investor who is hands-off as far as the day-to-day business is concerned. Ask how each investor works with their current clients – hands-on, hands-off, or somewhere in the middle.

Other filtering questions might include: Who are some of your other investments? Are you local? In which industries do you specialize? Are you a solo investor or in a group? What type of client do you prefer? Am I your type of client?

By doing your due diligence, you reduce the risk of having to break up with your new investor sooner than planned.

Building trust takes time and an investment from both parties. At the end of a successful pitch to gain an investor, the trust clock starts ticking. You both must deliver now on the promises made during the courtship; nothing builds trust faster than doing what you said you would do. And when you follow through, the role of trusted advisor just naturally evolves.

9: Demonstrating Credibility

So far, I have talked about general tools that you need to have in place to pitch effectively, such as your execution roadmap, organizational infrastructure, financial reporting, and relationships with potential investors.

Before we go on, examine this infographic to better understand the seven essential tools you must acquire before you can tell your company's story through executive summaries and pitch decks.

Figure 5: Infographic – Foundational Tools Come First

The 7 Essential Tools to Raise Capital

	What	When	How
1	Execution Road Map	Every stage of the business, beginning with the idea.	Strategically helps the team stay on track and helps you show milestones reached with investors and future initiatives.
2	Infrastructure	Every stage of the business, beginning with the idea.	CRM, General Ledger, billing software, operations systems, documented processes and procedures. Use these to make strategic decisions and to accumulate data to pitch.
3	Cash requirements and Burn Rate	Every stage of the business, beginning with the idea.	You need this to run the business as well as pitch to investors.
4	Database of Investors	Every stage of the business, beginning with the idea.	Start & routinely maintain a list of investors, their specific interest and notes from your conversations. This could prove to be invaluable during the building of your business, as you can specifically target the right investor.
5	One Page Executive Summary	Introductory stage with investor.	When you initially meet an investor and you want to send them information to get their attention.
6	Pitch Deck to email	ONLY after a potential investors request.	This Pitch Deck stands on its own and presents the key elements the investor will be interested in knowing.
7	Pitch Deck to Present	When are you Pitching?!	This Pitch Deck needs to serve as a backdrop for your speech and should not stand alone without you. You want the audience focused on you and what you are saying.

Every entity needs to maintain a certain amount of infrastructure and data to manage the business, as well as to be ready to present to investors and/or provide for due diligence in the event of a sale. Growing entities often forget about maintaining information such as numbers of customers in the sales funnel, number of presentations to customers and the close rate from presentations, number of active customers, lapse of customers (including reasons why they lapsed), and average revenue dollars per customer. These numbers may sound simple to maintain, but let me share some of my journeys to pin down some of these simple metrics.

Metrics and Credibility

I was hired on a Friday by an investor to get an entrepreneur ready to pitch to investors the following Tuesday. I asked the founder/entrepreneur to send me the projections, the active customer list, and the list of customers he had lost over the three years he had been in business. He sent the first two pieces of information right away, and then when I asked again for a list of customers he had lost, he said he had not lost any. This sounded odd – but okay, I decided to take that statement at face value.

I began reviewing his existing pitch deck and the information it contained. He had numbers and projections on the number of customers he anticipated over the next five years; however, there was nothing about the current number of customers or the average revenue per customer. I began my analytical process with the data and calculated the average revenue per customer. Surprised it was a very low number per customer, I went to the website to review the pricing for the product. It was much higher than the average per customer price. Then I began to look at the customer list further and the dates they were added on as a customer. I recognized one of the names of the customer and it was near my home – further it had a "closed and out of business" sign on the front and had been out of business for a very long time. I reached out to the founder and asked about the customer. He was shocked they had an out of business sign and said the business had paid their invoice. I further investigated the cash receipts and noticed the entity had not paid in two years, which led to further analysis of the cash receipts from the customer list. From this, I was able to determine they had indeed lost customers, with a churn (loss) rate of approximately

10 percent per year – which is bad. The fact that this founder was about to go into a pitch to tell the potential investors that he had never lost a customer when it was not true – horrible. When the investors began their due diligence, they would learn the business did have customer churn, and the founder would have lost credibility.

Furthermore, if the founder and his team had been paying closer attention to when and how customers paid, they would have realized the customer was past due. A follow-up email or phone call may have collected further revenue or even resulted in a potential up-sale for a new product feature. One of the best in the industry at this tactic is DropBox. When you are coming close to your annual renewal with DropBox, you will think you are the hottest thing since the homecoming queen at your high school, as they will send you email after email about your upcoming renewal and the features you are missing out on. This past year during the renewal process, I felt like I had to learn a new language to know about their offerings and determine how the potential new features would impact my business. Going back to my founder – the customer that had gone out of business had received almost two years of the service for free. All the cost incurred with delivering the product continued to be incurred by the company. It lost the revenue but never received the cash receipts.

One of my former clients had purchased a company with a base of business and a technology platform they anticipated would be easy to grow. As the founders worked on growing the business, they discovered the technology needed almost a complete overhaul. They hired a development team and began the process of building a new product. The customers established on the vintage product had typically renewed annually, and with the focus on the new product, the vintage customers were addressed only when they called the customer service line. The founders had every intention of reaching out to these customers and selling them on the new product, but it never really happened. Within a short period of time, the customers discovered the same limitations of the vintage product and began to seek alternatives. They explored the internet and talked to others and found new products. The founders continued to count each of these customers as existing customers and would even say during their pitch to investors that they anticipated upselling the customers on the new product. The fact is, they never really tried. It turns out that when they eventually sent out invoices for the annual renewal, they learned customers had switched to another product for functionality and, in most cases, a product that competed with theirs. So back to pitching to investors, and my point – they were counting customers who were not using the product, they were missing out on an opportunity to upsell, and they were misleading investors. Had they implemented a process to reach out to customers at least once a quarter to engage with them personally, they would have had a better chance of retaining them.

Infrastructure is about systems and process. People run the systems and process, so they are part of the equation, as well. Leaders of organizations often say they cannot afford a monthly subscription for a software like a CRM, expense management, or bill pay system. When you are in front of a group of investors and they begin to ask you questions about the metrics of your business, how will you feel admitting, "I don't know because I didn't pay a few dollars a month for the software to maintain the data"? Get in front of a mirror right now and say that to your face. If you can't say that with confidence and pride, then make the commitment right now to set up infrastructure. I know what I would do.

The purpose of this story was to show how taking shortcuts can sell you short in the long run. As you entered the world of entrepreneurship, your goals were more likely focused on putting one foot in front of the other to set up shop and pay the bills. Critical infrastructure and solid processes were lower on the list of priorities and never seemed to make it to the top. One of my goals in this book is to convince you to find the time and resources to move those initiatives to the top of the priority list, especially if your endgame will ever be to raise capital or sell your business.

10: Building the Perfect Pitch

The Pitch Decks – Why You Need Two

The creation and management of your pitch deck is a critical part of the capital-raising process and deserves its own chapter. While you are networking with potential investors, you may be asked to send your pitch deck via email or present it to a group of investors. If your response is something like, "Let me put it together and get back to you in a couple of weeks," you can probably write off that potential investor, as they will move on to other projects and entrepreneurs who *are ready to take their money*. You need to keep both pitch decks always up to date.

As alluded to above, you will need two different pitch decks. I refer to the more detailed version as Pitch Deck #1, the Handout Pitch Deck. This version stands alone and doesn't rely on your verbal explanation of the content.

Pitch Deck #2 is the Presentation Pitch Deck. This version does rely on you delivering your pitch, aided by high-level slides with few words and lots of images.

Remember, this is a sales presentation. You are presenting to people who have limited time or who may just be high-strung and have a very intense case of ADHD, i.e. a short attention span. It just comes with the territory. The opportunity to pitch is not the time to go into every little small detail about how the lemonade stand you had when you were in second grade helped you become an entrepreneur. Get to the business of what they want to know – what is your business about and how can it make enough money to return multiples of the amount of money they want to invest. I'm going to reveal the key elements of information critical to your 10-slide pitch presentation. This chapter includes an outline and description for developing Pitch Deck #1, which is the one you will email investors when asked for a copy. Then, using the first slide deck, you will develop Pitch Deck #2, the "show" you will use when you present to investors. That pitch deck will have very few words and numbers, if any; instead, it will function much like a television or movie screen, and the audience will focus on you rather than trying to read.

The Handout Pitch Deck must quickly communicate your "Why me?" to potential investors. If you have followed my recommendations, you have already researched (or paid someone to discover) which investors will invest in your space and what they will ask when they are getting ready to invest. Keep the content of Pitch Deck #1 refreshed so you can distribute it at a moment's notice. Just as every professional has an up-to-date resume to present at any time, a growing entrepreneurial company should have both pitch decks ready to email or present at any time.

Figure 6: Comparison of the Two Pitch Decks

Slide	Presentation Deck	Email/Handout Deck
Cover Page	Logo, Company Name, Presenter Name, Position/Title	Logo and Company Name
Business Overview	A picture that tells the story of the business	Should describe this in as few words as possible
The Team	Professional descriptions of your team, including embellishments, such as any Fortune 100 they may have worked for	Professional descriptions of your team
Bottom-Up Market View	An estimate of potential sales to determine a total sales figure displayed in graphic form	An estimate of potential sales to determine a total sales figure – more quantitative analysis than presentation deck
Product Information	Name of the product and a picture of it	Name and short description of the product
Business Model	Key point of the pitch – How is the investment going to pay off and how will you know?	Short description of your business strategy to benefit from the investment
Competition	Show the logos of your	Format information

Slide	Presentation Deck	Email/Handout Deck
	competition, and illustrate the attributes of your product vs your competition	as a grid showing the attributes of your company's product vs. those of the competition
Financial Overview	An analysis of the projected income statement	Same information
The Ask	Be specific about how much money you are asking for and the use of funds	Same information
Wrap-Up	Your contact information and time for questions	Company website and contact information

Get Psyched to Deliver Your Pitch

Make sure if you are the presenter that you have prepared and feel your "superhero best" on the day of the presentation. That's my cousin in the following photo – Captain America – along with his colleagues of the non-profit Heroes In Force[4], which helps brighten the day for children who are in hospitals or are ill. He made his costume.

Figure 7: Bring your Superhero Persona to Deliver your Pitch!

Photo by Crystal Sims Hembree, used with permission.

Back to you – If you have been asked to present, ask a few questions when the date and time are confirmed. Ask if the investor has a template they would like you to follow, and if the answer is yes, use it. I have seen many who have decided to ignore the template, which is not a good idea. You generally start off irritating the investor by not following their request.

Ask how much time you have and prepare to stay on track for the time frame.

Ask who will be in the room and do research about their background. You perhaps can determine if they worked with your competitors and already understand the business. Perform in-depth research and, if possible, talk to others who know them. Determine what their average investment amount is and if it is in the ballpark of what you seek. The more you learn about their background, the better you can tailor the discussion to them.

Make sure the day or so before the presentation that you exercise and eat right, get plenty of sleep, and do what it takes to build up your confidence and energy. Make sure you are extremely careful about the phone calls you take the day before. Your friend who calls to complain about her cheating spouse and cries for hours needs to find another emotional sounding board the night before your presentation. Your family and support group need to know that 24 hours before your presentation is not the right time to go over the data on the cell phone plan, put the toilet paper on backward, forget to let the dog out, and other things that can drive you crazy.

The day of the presentation, you should arrive early and go in the bathroom and or somewhere private before the presentation and meditate, do your yoga stretches, or stand in your superwoman/superman stance – whatever works for you to get your psyche ready to pitch.

Make sure you are professionally dressed. I recently sat in on a series of pitches with a group of investors, and although they liked one of the companies and chose to move forward with due diligence, they did comment that the presenter had dressed unprofessionally. He had on the hoodie sweatshirt, blue jeans, and tennis shoes. Business casual with a jacket is a safe bet for these presentations.

Use the following template for both pitch decks, and I will discuss the differences between the two after I talk about the basic guts of each one.

Pitch Deck Content Details

Key aspects of a successful pitch deck are conciseness, professionalism, and visual appeal. Use these guidelines to build the content of the deck. Engage your marketing team to add the template background, images, and pizzazz.

<u>Slide 1 – Cover Page.</u> Simple, crisp, and clean is the key for this page. Make sure you have a dynamite, knock-your-socks-off, high-resolution logo. I cannot stand to see a fuzzy, low-res logo on the cover page; this smacks of laziness and lack of attention to detail. Don't doom your presentation at the outset by causing the potential investor not to take you seriously.

If you are presenting in person, add your name and position with the company. Do not put your picture, your entire résumé, or other wordy content – just your name and position. Nothing more. You want the audience to focus on you, your confident superhero self, and what you are saying, instead of trying to read something on the slide.

<u>Slide 2 – Business Overview – Why?</u> On this slide answer these questions:

→ What is the business?

→ What problem does it solve for the customer?

→ Timing – why now?

The Pitch Deck you email should describe this in as few words as possible. The Pitch Deck for the presentation should have a picture that tells the story of the business. You need your marketing and creative geniuses to work on this with you. Consider showing a picture of the business depicting a product being manufactured or service being delivered. A picture of a building or a conference room won't cut it.

<u>Slide 3 – The Team.</u> Make sure you highlight your team members professionally. If you have a team member who worked at Google, Facebook, Amazon, or any other highly-recognizable name, use their logo on this slide. Concisely describe everyone's background. The point here is to demonstrate you have the team who can effectively use investment dollars to deliver the growth you both need to succeed. Remember, this is all about an investment!

Slide 4 – Bottom-up Market View. Discuss the market with a bottom-up approach. Calculate a **bottom-up** analysis by estimating individual potential sales to determine a total sales figure. A bottom-up analysis takes into consideration where products can be sold, the sales of comparable products, and current sales you can predict. This approach is comprehensive and accurate.

In comparison, the **top-down** approach looks like this: there are millions of females in the world, and if we project one half of one percent will purchase our product, we will meet our goals. At the likely risk of losing all credibility, do not start off the market discussion with this type of comment.

Your goal is to demonstrate that you understand the market you are going after and your ability to penetrate it. If your market is too small, you will not be able to make money, product or pricing notwithstanding. Mention the market size briefly and have more in-depth data prepared if asked, usually the details you generated to arrive at your summary illustration about market size.

Recently I attended a Venture Conference where companies were pitching to a large audience dominated by investors. One company stood out because it just did not seem to fit in with the technology and software-as-a-service entrepreneurs. This company sold a boring product; but they had fine-tuned their pitch so that as they presented, I became intrigued to learn more about...cat litter! Their slide showing the market had a lot of visual appeal paired with great information for potential investors. I was so intrigued by their pitch that I left the presentation and purchased their product. I must agree this cat litter is superior to the basic brands on the market and makes a nasty experience the best it can be.

Slide 5 – Product Information. This seems like a no-brainer, but...you have already talked about the business, now you need to drill down to the product. Don't be so intertwined with your company and your business you forget to add to the pitch deck the name of the product(s) you are selling. I can tell you I have seen many pitch decks where the name of the product was nowhere to be found.

<u>Slide 6 – Business Model.</u> Describing your business model is essential. Amazon, Uber, and other unicorns have invested unprecedented amounts of money to gain market share. When you look at the core business principles applied to these business models, they may resemble gambling more than a business model; yet for these companies, it paid off. There are those businesses that warrant a speed-to-market approach and investing dollars to gain market share; SaaS (software as a service) companies are a good example.

Gaining market share is where a financial strategy is essential when building a business. If you consciously decide to build a business by heavily investing in gaining customers, you must budget the investment and monitor it for effectiveness. If you foolishly spend money in the name of "investing in the business," without a clear path showing how the investment is going to pay off, you are acting irresponsibly. By monitoring metrics like the cost to acquire a customer, the monthly burn rate, and the number of employees, you can monitor actual results, adjusting your financial strategy if one path isn't paying off as planned.

The business model slide should also demonstrate you have command of how you are going to build this business to generate a profit. Address the cost of your product in a manner that shows the cost today versus the cost as you scale up the business. Your audience will expect you to address how you are going to continue to produce your product or service and distribute it during a high growth cycle. Information they look for includes an analysis of the cost of goods sold, including commission cost. The dollars invested in acquiring customers should be well-thought-out and communicated to the investor. The general and administrative costs to run the day-to-day-business – including the salaries of the C-Suite, IT, and accounting department and operations – should be included and analyzed. The way you set up your financial infrastructure and manage as you acquire customers will determine if you can scale effectively. For example, one accounts receivable clerk may be able to handle ten customers with a highly manual and easy-to-follow process. A single clerk will not be able to manually handle billing and collections for hundreds or thousands of customers.

Here is an example of bad infrastructure that affected me personally, and which led to bad cash flow.

My daughter attended a small private school where we used my husband's GI Bill benefits to pay for a portion of the tuition for the first two years. The third year, when the tuition bill came, it showed the offset of the GI Bill. I called and told the college it was a mistake; the offset shouldn't carry over in year three. They argued with me and tried to convince me I was wrong. Three times, I tried unsuccessfully to tell them they were incorrect. I finally gave up. You can probably guess the conclusion: a year later they contacted me, telling me there was a mistake and they would have to bill me for the tuition. Because of their mistake, they lost the benefit of the revenue due to their bad infrastructure. I would argue they grew too fast and failed to manage and monitor the infrastructure they needed to grow at that pace.

If you are selling a high-specialty product like homemade brownies, a unique software, or high-end cosmetics that extract ingredients from unique and hard-to-find plants – you may have the best product in the world, and your clients may love it. How are you going to build a scalable business around these types of products? How are you going to make enough of the products? Are you going to hire enough people and train them? Are you going to rent warehouse space to store them? How are you going to package the product so it will arrive at your customer's destination intact? How are you going to coordinate shipping, and will you charge the customer or absorb the shipping cost in the price of the product?

Here is a new one – how are you going to deal with the increasing regulatory rules, including dealing with the interstate sales tax? The recent Supreme Court ruling in Wayfair vs. South Dakota means that states can require online retailers to collect sales tax, regardless if they have a physical presence in the state.

The point is this: substantiate projections that show significant growth in revenue with a business model that will support the growth.

This problem exists for small and large businesses. I work with businesses frequently involved in upgrading their general ledger software. There are a few large giants in this industry that have experienced exponential growth and have purchased smaller software companies to grow faster. Some of these giants are delivering horrible service. They have grown too fast and have failed to integrate the new acquisitions successfully. The wait time to get through to customer service is long. Once you get through, the person you get on the phone often does not know the answer to the problem.

The best recent example of an issue with a business model, and one that is so easy to understand, is Movie Pass, a movie ticket subscription service. Movie Pass sold monthly memberships for $9 to see unlimited movies at a theater. The Movie Pass Company paid movie theaters nearly full price for tickets. With the national average price of a movie at just under $9, it did not take long for the Movie Pass Company to have cash flow issues. In July 2018, ticket-takers denied Movie Pass holders entrance to movie theaters. It turns out Movie Pass had run out of money and could not pay the movie theaters. Movie Pass took out an emergency loan and doubled the monthly subscription price.[5] The debt they took on was very expensive debt, and with a losing business model in the first place, it is difficult to see how they are going to raise enough money to make even more money. Every time I read an article about this, my head spins a bit and I get nervous. Then I remember – whew, it is not my money!

The difference between the pitch deck you send via email and the one you present to potential investors is generally this: the email version will show more specific numbers about the cost of goods sold and other expenses. When you are presenting, you will turn those numbers into a visual and discuss the big picture overall. You will need to know (and have the supporting details for) the numbers you use in the big picture, but do not include these detailed numbers on the slides.

Slide 7 – Competition. Never ever say you have no competition. Every business has competition in some way. A successful business solves a problem for its customer. Convincing an investor your company has the only solution to the problem is like when a teenager breaks up with a first love, convinced he or she will never find love again. It is just not a realistic thought.

Conduct a thorough analysis of your competition. The internet is a great resource for free information. When you are pitching your product to a potential investor, ask questions about other investment options they are considering. You need to do this in the sales process, but it is also an incredible tool for research to help with the macro-strategy of the business. Potential investors ask all the time what companies you lose business to and why. Your curiosity as an emotionally intelligent leader should lead you to want to grow your business properly. If you do not know the answer when investors ask this, you will lose credibility. To be thorough, consider subscribing to a site where you can delve into deeper details using business intelligence acquired by professional researchers. Examples of these types of sites include Reuters, LexisNexis, and TechCrunch.

I worked with a very early stage startup that thought they had no competition, and that their AI (Artificial Intelligence) solution was the only one in existence. My research team located a very well-funded international company with the same type of technology, who would present as a very fierce competitor. They had already established infrastructure and marketing efforts to sell worldwide. This discovery was one of the issues that halted the planned multi-million-dollar capital raise to launch a company for their AI product.

Now that I have convinced you to call out your competition, be very careful to analyze your product and service against the competition. Highlight your unique value proposition and the value you bring to your client as to how you can solve their problem better than the competition.

The format for the pitch deck you email should be a grid showing the attributes of your company's product versus those of the competition. Your illustration should include a list of your strongest and most competitive features, as compared to your top three to four competitors.

When formatting the Competition slide for your pitch deck, include the logos of your competition and illustrations of your product vs. theirs. Talk about the most important unique values of your product and why it's better than the other guy's, in the order of the most important. Include stories of how you won customers over the competition. As an example, QuickBooks wins clients over Zero and FreshBooks because there are more accounting professionals trained on its product than the other two. This is a large part of its strategy to maintain their market share. QuickBooks provides easy access to free training for accountants to learn its product.

Slide 8 – Financial Overview. This slide is different than the Business Model, in that it is an overall big picture view of the financials. They need to both be very high level and match the detailed financial projections you have prepared that have the projected income statement and EBITDA for five years. This slide will include four rows maximum and a large font. Make sure when you have the presentation up you can read the content from the back of the room.

Slide 9 – The Ask. Here it is – the reason you are here. You want something from them, and it's time to ask for it. Be specific about how much money you are asking for and the use of funds. Do not say we are raising money and need a range of $1 million to $5 million. You will lose credibility instantly. Show the use of funds at a very high level; for example, if you are using the money to hire staff, do not list every position you plan to hire in the presentation, but be prepared to talk about it.

If you have read my book, conducted research, and developed your strategy, you should already know the range the investor is willing to invest in each of their investments. Use that information to tailor your comments as you speak to the investor, and make sure it aligns with the amount you are asking for. If you need $2 million but know this investor typically invests $1 million, they may be able to invest with another firm that can supply the additional $1 million to get to the $2 million you need.

Slide 10 – Wrap-up. The last slide should contain your contact information and "Questions?" Leave this slide up as long as possible while your presentation wraps up, so your contact information is apparent.

Once you have a good DRAFT of the presentation, practice, practice, practice. Get your trusted advisors and professional acquaintances who know little about your business to listen to your pitch. This is the group who will ask questions similar to what you can expect from investors.

Use those who know your business to ensure you are highlighting it accurately. I have worked with founders and entrepreneurs who casually describe their business, yet when I see their pitch, their unique value proposition is not even mentioned. This happens because you get so entrenched in your business, you cannot see the trees for the forest. Use your trusted advisors to help you find the trees.

Finally, in preparation for the live presentation, watch this YouTube video at least once as you prepare to present: "The Origin of the WHY" by Simon Sinek (YouTube, 12/15/2016).[6] Even if you are 10,000 percent comfortable with your Why, make sure you can communicate it as passionately as he does in this video. It is a great demonstration of how to communicate about your company in a passionately infectious way to capture and hold the attention of potential investors and clients – so you can sell your product.

11: Put a Bow On It

Now that we have finished the nuts and bolts of the pitch preparation and process, here are some additional tips to help you along the way.

Make certain you have the right trusted advisors. Your team should also include:

- ✓ The right CPA firm advising you on tax issues
- ✓ A great attorney to help you set up your corporate structure and maintain your corporate records
- ✓ A financial professional who can provide you with real-time financial records and analysis

After the pitch, if there is interest from the investors, execute a confidentiality agreement or a non-disclosure agreement, if you have not already done so. There should be a Letter of Intent ("LOI") signed by both parties as soon as practical. Insist on a time frame for the closing date of the investment. You do not want to take your company off the market for months only to have the investor back out. Use the terms of the LOI to motivate a quick decision.

As you have read in previous chapters, getting ready to find an investor begins long before you think you will need the money. Preparations include thinking through how to build a business that investors will want to invest in, and one with which they can identify. You must maintain credible data on your financials and your potential client base so each time you meet with an investor, you can confidently communicate your position.

How confident are you in your preparation of accurate historical and projected financials? If the right investor were to come along, could you demonstrate a thorough knowledge of the financials, cash flow, burn rate, use of proceeds, and return on investment? Knowing your product inside and out, as well as the financial numbers behind it, is crucial. Expect to be drilled on this type of information when you meet with investors. It will feel like the worst spelling bee you ever participated in if you are not prepared, and savvy investors will smell your fear. Do you feel confident?

Items to consider in determining if your business is ready for investment:

Is the product fully functioning and completely tested? If not, the due diligence process will uncover this undesirable state.

Have you sold a company before? If yes, even if it was not completely successful, this fact will help you with the pitch, as you have experience. Share your successes as well as your failures and how you have learned from them.

Do you and the C-Suite have substantial experience and a strong reputation in the industry, including big-name contacts in your field? This fact will most certainly assist with the process of making a credible pitch.

Are you happy to earn a modest salary during the next few years of growth? Investors do not want to pay for you to put your child through college or for your vacation home. They want to fund aggressive growth and then share with you the rewards of that growth.

If you have raised money before, use this to your advantage; it shows you have already successfully completed the process.

Have you demonstrated, with your cash flow projection and burn rate, your ability to invest the money and turn the enterprise cash flow positive within the time frame you are presenting within the pitch deck?

Is the C-Suite aligned with the proposed strategy and execution? I have seen time and again a management team debate, in front of their potential investor, how they will accomplish the projected growth. This is a sure-fire recipe for failure.

Are you keenly aware of your competition and how they will react to your success? One exercise that can yield useful insight is to discuss with your C-Suite by asking, "If you were the CEO of our competition, how would you react to the growth I plan to execute?" What will it mean to you, and how will you react to their reaction? Important think tank sessions are essential to plan growth strategically.

The process of pitching to investors is a lot like parenting. You cannot read a book and know everything you need to know. Each child and each investor are unique and require a different approach and strategy.

The good news is the core attributes of getting ready to pitch to investors are, for the most part, in your control and are what you need to run your business day-to-day anyway. I challenge you to make sure you are building the right kind of infrastructure for both reasons.

If you are this far along in the book, you are probably already somewhere on the journey. I wish you the best and invite you to work on self-improvement and self-awareness along the way. Business owners and their leadership are critical to the success of a company as it grows; this same team is essential to the success of a pitch for investment dollars.

Works Cited

[1] Matthew Boyle. "Target to Buy Shipt for $550 Million in Challenge to Amazon," Bloomberg. December 13, 2017. https://www.bloomberg.com/news/articles/2017-12-13/target-to-buy-shipt-for-550-million-in-bet-on-same-day-delivery

[2] Benjamin Raines. "Investors Shouldn't Panic About Amazon's PillPack Purchase," June 28. 2018. www.nasdaq.com/article/investors-shouldnt-panic-about-amazons-pillpack-purchase-cm985088

[3] Jenny Edelston. "Roche to Acquire Flatiron Health to Accelerate Industry-Wide Development and Delivery of Breakthrough Medicines for Patients with Cancer," February 15, 2018. https://flatiron.com/press/press-release/roche

[4] Heroes In Force is a nonprofit dedicated to equipping and empowering children, youth, and adults to "Be the Hero" in their schools, work, community and lives. Their website is www.heroesinforce.com for more information or to donate.

[5] Carrie Wittmer. "MoviePass is experiencing technical difficulties again, days after it ran out of money and had to borrow $5 million in cash," Business Insider. July 29, 2018. https://www.businessinsider.my/moviepass-is-down-again-days-after-it-ran-out-of-money-2018-7

[6] Sinek, Simon. "The Origin of the WHY," December 15, 2016. Video file. https://www.youtube.com/watch?v=nRaqe9M2DYc